Published By: Pen Legacy®

Cover By: Christian Cuan

Edited By: U Can Mark My Word Editorial Services

Formatting By: Junnita Jackson

Library of Congress Cataloging – in- Publication Data has been applied for.

ISBN: 978-1-7354580-2-1

PRINTED IN THE UNITED STATES OF AMERICA.

Table of Contents

INTRODUCTION

Whether or not we admit our truths, we all have experienced some form of traumatic events that have resulted in us being left feeling numb, broken, confused, or doubtful. Some experiences have even caused us to develop toxic characteristics. The types of traumatic events include, but are not limited to:

- sexual and physical abuse/assault
- war or political violence
- emotional and mental abuse
- psychological maltreatment
- neglect
- serious accident or severe illness
- medical procedure
- grief
- system-induced trauma
- forced displacement
- and bullying.

As we go through life, we tend to mask our pain and suppress our feelings. However, if we peel back the layer of our outer image, our true inner selves will be revealed. Each of us has faced a season in our lives that we believed with all certainty would break us or like we wouldn't survive. You may even feel as though you are presently in the midst of that season.

The one thing you must remember is that you are not alone. We all have a story, and our stories of trauma, challenges, pain, and setbacks should be told. When we develop the strength and courage to face our truths, it is then that we are able to free ourselves from captivity and begin our healing journey. We gain our identity and own who we are, thereby discovering our purpose and empowering ourselves to inspire, embrace, and heal others.

In Put a Nail, End It, our co-authors share their stories of living in their truth unapologetically, embracing vulnerability, and removing their mask of hurt, shame, and guilt. The authors come armed with their stories of being completely raw, authentic, and transparent with you. By being transparent, they acknowledge their traumatic events and toxic characteristics in order to arrive at a place of healing, growing, glowing, and evolving in their purpose.

As you begin reading, you will be inspired by how these authors have turned their experiences into victories instead of playing the victim. They have turned their test into a testimony. It's time to make a change and unlock your confidence! It's time to put an end to your fears and soar in your faith! After reading Put a Nail, End It, the co-authors and

I hope you are inspired, encouraged, and empowered to inspire someone else. Step out of your comfort zone and evolve into who God destined you to be!

Kiawana "Key" Leaf

Bettina M. Brown grew up a military brat and was privileged to see the moon from the other side of the world. With a great deal of patience, love, and God, Bettina decided that instead of accepting the trauma she was subjected to, she would turn those things into positives by taking her trauma and using it to create a message of hope for others. In 2019, Bettina created a podcast entitled "In the Rising" that gives her the platform to talk about her professional and personal life. She discusses how self-acceptance will improve your relationship with yourself and others. Bettina has plans to publish her manuscript in 2020. Bettina has found fulfillment in life through her spiritual walk with the Creator.

DRINKING FROM THE CORRECT LIFE-CHANGING CUP

What they never tell you about growing up is that sometimes you will find yourself hanging by your fingertips. Fighting to stop the muscles from trembling so you don't fall. Trying not to lose the thing that we think is most important in the world. The stressors of life become your nemesis. Something as insignificant as having your mop bucket stolen can have you spiraling out of control. Yes, at my lowest point, even my mop bucket being taken took me from zero to a thousand in six seconds. Then, there may come a time when the weight of the world becomes just too much for you to carry. You may find yourself lying on the tile floor of your bathroom in a fetal position, unable to move.

You are cordially invited to my story—my message of hope from my bad experiences and my testimony from the tests, if you will, that I had to endure. I had just moved to

Albuquerque, New Mexico, a city that had finally banned the show COPS from filming as it affected tourism. Albuquerque is located in the middle of the state and home of the University of New Mexico, where I had decided to attend graduate school. My parents drove the scenic three-hour drive and helped me find a studio apartment. They set up the apartment with all the basics, and I felt like a kid going away to college. During my undergraduate years, I lived at home. My father said I should make sure never to take a step backward and move back home. I had to follow my dream of becoming a physical therapist and make this work in Albuquerque.

With all the unpacking, moving, and decorating, our stomachs began to tighten from hunger pains, and we opted to go to Einstein Bros. Bagels. This bagel shop was close to my place, and it was open. I ordered plain cream cheese on a toasted plain bagel, with lots of honey drizzled on top. As I attempted to pay the cashier for my order, I focused on trying not to stare at him. He had his tongue split in the middle, tattoos on the side of his neck, fake horns inserted just above his forehead. This all was accentuated with a dyed red Mohawk, complete with perfect spikes.

My father leaned in and said, "You know what? I take it back. I can take you back home." I chuckled while looking at my father. No, I was going to make this work.

One month later, my "making it work" began to get tested. My parents decided to split up after decades of marriage. The who, what, when, and why is not important, but the fact that our family was now separated was devastating. While listening to the news from my parents over the telephone, I went numb with shock, and my chest tightened. Even in my 20's, a change like this was still heartbreaking.

One week later, I began Human Anatomy and had to muster the stomach to begin the cadaver lab. For nearly ten minutes, my stomach twisted and turned before we went into the lab. We were warned it would be hard, and it was. Each student had to fight the smell of death. The odor of formaldehyde penetrates your skin, while the sounds of body bags zipping open and closed stays with you always. We had to train our minds to know that if we wanted to help others, our first act was to decimate a body to learn its workings. We were to investigate the human body—memorizing muscles, ligaments, and nerves to produce correct answers on weekly quizzes. Each student was also given a black bone box filled with human bones, where were boiled down to remove all traces of tissue. We were required to study the contents and better learn the feel of boney landmarks. I brought the box home to my studio apartment, which happened to face a cemetery, and I cannot even begin to describe the dreams I had each night that summer.

To make matters worse, this was also the year we had a moth outbreak in the city. Moths would be waiting to attack when you pulled toilet paper from the roll. Turning off the light didn't offer relief from the moths, as the superspecies constantly fluttered while looking for ways to escape. I finally left the radio on at night so I could not hear them flying into the walls.

Partially through the summer, I received a phone call from a cousin. My grandmother had passed away, and it was my job to notify my father. I called him and tried to be gentle with my words, and through the phone line, it seemed as though he took the news okay. But, I didn't. It was so incredibly hard to tell that sobering news to my father. That night, I drank more than one glass of wine.

I continued to go to the lab and was getting used to the process, until we were given a memorable lecture. Whenever someone found an anomaly with their cadaver, we would all gather around as a class. A group of classmates had discovered something was "different" in the abdomen of their subject. Cancer. I got to see what the disease can do to the body. And the fact that my godmother had just passed away six months before I started school brought home another loss. That night, I had several more glasses of wine.

The summer turned into fall, and then came the day. I woke up on my birthday, feeling alone. It was the first year that I was alone on my birthday. There was no cake, no singing, and I felt isolated. I tried to make the best of it and continued with my day.

Later that night, I got together with a group of friends. We met at a small place called Gecko's off Central Boulevard, part of the original Route 66 highway. Central Boulevard is heaven for people watchers who are eager to see all walks of life passing by. That night, I drank heavily and became part of the scenery instead of being a spectator. I wanted so much to numb my pain that I kept drinking. At some point, I decided that getting my ear pierced was the thing to do, and I was in luck. There was a tattoo and piercing shop next to the bar. However, a classmate of mine didn't think it was the best idea because of the amount of alcohol I had consumed. "It thins the blood, Bettina," they had said. I was not to be stopped, though. I was so inebriated that I could only manage to sign an "X" for my signature after swiping my debit card, accessing the student loan funds in my account.

An upscale place wouldn't have accepted an "X" as my signature or did the piercing with me being intoxicated. It was my good fortune that I was not in such a place, and they went forth with the piercing. To say that I bled would be an understatement. I just kept bleeding. It took at least an hour before the bleeding turned into the past tense of bled. I don't know what happened after that.

The following day, I insisted on going to school since there was a strict attendance policy, and as it should be. After all, we were graduate students, each investing tens of thousands of dollars to be healthcare providers. In hindsight, I should have skipped school. That day in class, I was an example of what not to do. I couldn't get onto the platform to be the subject and couldn't off the platform to be the treating therapist without running to the bathroom. Everything kept swimming around me until well into the afternoon. Even though it was embarrassing, I am glad that I went, because I realized my drinking was covering up hurt and grief. I just had to push through. I didn't want to let anyone see me so depressed.

My drinking continued to affect my finances, and I was robbing Peter to pay Paul to pay my bills. My situation would have been bleak even without my expenditures on alcohol. I paid all my bills and credit cards. Well, actually, that is not true. I did not pay one credit card. I had to wait until loan disbursement to continue payment. I kept avoiding their phone calls until I finally answered one day. That's when I learned I had to pay the entire nine thousand dollars now. They had closed the account and wanted their money. Devastated, I sat on the floor and cried.

I had nothing left to give them. I recited the entire story to him, treating the call like a mini counseling session for myself. The credit card representative had no idea what he was getting into when he dialed my number. I cried to the point that I sobbed, and I had trouble collecting a single breath. I was full of emotion and tears, and my eyes burned incredibly.

After some time of being very quiet, he finally said, "Ma'am, may I pray with you?"

I thought I had heard wrong. After the fog that I had slipped into cleared a bit, I felt the word "yes" escape from my lips, and he prayed powerfully over me and for me. He had compassion, yet strength and sternness. He made it clear that I would make it through my emotional circumstances and that I needed to focus on what brought me to Albuquerque in the first place. He prayed for several more minutes and then proceeded to set me up on a payment plan that would last six years. That day when I hung up the phone, I knew I needed more than myself. If a debt collector was praying for me, I was clearly in a lot of trouble. The following Sunday, I went to a Lutheran church that was within walking distance of where I lived. My timing was perfect. The pastor preached my sermon that day; it was my message to hear.

The pastor had a peaceful presence about her, as she stood in white in front of the congregation. With her hands clasped together, she slowly walked from one side of the church to the other, leaning to each side for an extended second.

She began the sermon with, "Sometimes the answer we get in life is no. No, we will not get that job. No, we may not get married. No, the diagnosis won't change. But, our answer every day to our Savior is yes. Yes, we will get out of bed, even if our hair is a mess. Yes, we go to school, even if we are too broken inside to take in the lesson. Yes, we get up."

Her sermon resonated with me, and I cried silently from beginning to the end. I didn't even stop crying as I walked out of the church. In fact, I cried the entire way home. I didn't have to beat myself up for not being perfect. I had to continue to say "yes."

I came home and rested somewhat comfortably on my futon. The mattress was so thin that I felt like I was lying directly on the railing. A few hours later, a classmate knocked at my door, holding a large bouquet. She said she knew I had been going through a lot and wanted to cheer me up. The flowers were beautiful and vibrant, but they did not come in a vase. Having never had flowers in that apartment, I didn't have a vase. Seeing that I was beginning to feel down about the fact that I had nothing to put the flowers in, my cheerful classmate walked into my bathroom and started rummaging around. Minutes later, she came out with the bouquet standing proudly in my toilet brush holder. To tell you the truth, it was perfect. When she was ready to leave, I walked her out, then turned around to lean over and pick up my mop bucket that was no longer there. I took it as a sign to stop trying to clean everything up. Just let it be.

I finished PT school, eventually bought a house, got married, and had my son. I also eventually got divorced and found myself back in financial trouble. However, when the pain began to boil over this time, I brought all the alcohol to my co-workers. I was not going to hide from any pain. We can't deal with what we refuse to feel. With much help, multiple jobs, and grace, I became financially clear three years later. I no longer hold on to life with trembling fingers but with clasped hands. I won't lie and say every moment is this way, because it is not. No, I still want to control things, but each time, I get a reminder that is not what this is all about. I am a child of God, and each lesson I learned might be for me or someone else. But, each dirty lesson must be faced with Him.

Ayaliah Smith is a 13-year-old middle school graduate who loves to laugh, bake, and listen to music. Ayaliah's favorite scripture is Philippians 4:13: "For I can do all things through Christ who strengthens me." She is the middle child of three from her mother and the only bundle of joy from her father.

OVERCOMING My Pain

On September 28, 2006, at 5:28 p.m. in Takoma Park, Maryland, the precious, beautiful baby girl Ayaliah was born. A special gift I was indeed, because the doctors didn't think I would make it. But God has the final word on everything. At just six weeks old, things were very challenging for me. I was barely able to breathe some days. Life for me was rocky, and I had many obstacles to overcome. However, the most important calamity was my health. I was told my father was sick at the time of my birth. We were both seeking treatment at the same time. Frequent trips to the doctor and hospital were the norm for us. I was approximately eight months old when my father became terminally ill, and he passed away before my first birthday.

When I was three months old, my health condition declined. I battled asthma and seizures at six months old. When I was fourteen months old, I underwent my first surgery. I had my adenoids and tonsils removed. Tubes were placed in my ears. I also had a cyst removed from my lungs. Life certainly wasn't great me.

As time passed, I wasn't getting any better, only worse. The hospital became a second home for me. With so many visits to the hospital, the nurses developed personal relationships with my mother and me. My constant visits to the hospital garnered me a special room filled with paintings picked just for me. When I was almost three years old, my ear infections became so severe that my left eardrum burst, and I had to have surgery to have tubes placed in my ear.

I started school a little while after the surgery. School was the beginning of fun for me. I loved my teachers and friends, and I was so spoiled that I was given extra blankets at naptime and could rest any place I wanted. I developed friendships with Demetrius and Jada, who later became my best friends. We were inseparable. We had playdates, and we always spent birthdays together. We had the same classes together until the third grade. It was my last year at the school, and I didn't want to leave. That school was all that I knew.

Third grade was a challenge for me, not because of school but because of my home life. I was always an honor roll student; no challenges there. This was the year my older sister, Aysa, turned sixteen. After her 16th birthday, she and my mother didn't get along very well; they always bumped heads. I think it's because they both are Aries and so much alike.

I looked up to my sister as my best friend and role model. Aysa was intelligent and beautiful. I mean, who wouldn't look up to her. My sister later went to live with her dad, and this change hurt me so bad. She still visited on the weekends, but it wasn't the same as living together. I had two other big sisters, Jourdan and Kiawana, but they were way older than me. I didn't think they would want to hang with me. One day, my sister and mother got into a huge fight, causing both sides of my family to become involved. I didn't get to see Aysa again for a long time after that. Because I was separated from my sister and felt like I had lost a part of me, I became rude and mean to people. My sister was my partner in crime; we were Thing 1 and Thing 2.

I didn't see Aysa for two and a half years. This separation hurt me deeply. I missed her terribly. My mother didn't know what I was going through because I never talked about my feelings with her. My behavior caused big problems in my family, leading to me not being able to see my father's side of the family. My mema was my heart and the only thing I had left of my dad. It hurt me not to see her. That's when I began to have suicidal thoughts and even made two attempts at ending my life. At the time, I felt it was the best choice for me. I never shared this with anyone, not even with my closest friend. I didn't see Aysa again until 2016.

Throughout my school years, I was bullied. Back then, anyone could get under my skin and hurt my feelings I changed schools in the fourth grade, and my eczema flared up bad, which resulted in the bullying getting worse. The kids I went to school with didn't know much about eczema, and they believed I was contagious. I only had one friend; I'll call her Kayla. Kayla didn't know me, but from the first day of school, she would always talk to me. No one knew me, what I had been through, and what health issues I was fighting. People thought because of my appearance that I wasn't hood, despite being raised in DC. They believed I was soft. Well, I was raised with class and respect, so I didn't fight or argue with girls unless provoked.

I went through a period where I believed everyone who talked to me wanted to be my friend. I soon learned that wasn't true. I know some of you can relate. I wanted to be one of the cool and popular females, but I felt like I didn't fit in. So, I started getting into trouble at school with my two friends, who I'll refer to as Niyla and Jayla. Niyla was two years older than me, and Jayla was one year older than me. One time, we got into a big altercation with one of Niyla's cousins, who went to our school, because she didn't like that we were the "it" girls. Sixth grade came around, and by then, I had matured a little and didn't get into trouble anymore. Those girls remained my friends because I felt they had been there for me when nobody else was; however, during that same year, Niyla, Jayla, and I fell off a little, even having a petty beef.

At the end of the school year, my mema passed away on May 14, 2018. During this time, we were doing end-of-the-year testing and activities. I was completely lost. I was just finding myself, and then I suddenly fell back into my old ways. Again, I tried to commit suicide, which I felt was my only escape. I really just wanted peace and not to see or talk to anyone. Suicidal thoughts were my way of grieving and dealing with the pain. I expressed myself by displaying bad habits and behaviors that weren't normal for me.

While dealing with the loss of my grandmother, my mother was diagnosed with cancer. All the bad things were happening to me at once, and I found myself asking God why. Why did I have to be sick and have so many obstacles in my way? But then, I remembered what my mother told me. She said, "God gives his toughest battles to his strongest soldiers." I have kept that in mind with everything I go through. My mindset now is that no battle is too tough for me to overcome after all I have already conquered.

During our seventh-grade year, Niyla, Jayla, and I settled our differences and became friends again. I didn't get in trouble as much as before from being around them. However, we now argued all the time about nothing. One particular time, we had a huge argument about how they became shady and envious of me. Niyla and Jayla became besties, and when they became besties, I felt a shift in our friendship. They became more distant from me. So, I started to keep my distance from them. As I distanced myself, we didn't associate with each other anymore whatsoever. We were no longer friends. During the school year, I noticed that every time I got up or presented something in class, they would whisper to each other and laugh. I went to the assistant principal and addressed this with her. She resolved the issue, but we still weren't friends.

When my sister left and my mother was diagnosed with cancer, I never knew what was going on. I was only nine years old! What does a nine-year-old really know about cancer? Well, I did know. I just acted like I didn't. When I started asking questions, I revealed to my family that I knew more than they thought I did. The weight of it all started to lift a bit off my shoulders. I didn't have to hide my feelings about my mother's situation anymore. Of course, I was hurt and scared because I was well aware of what cancer did to the patient. I always thought, Wow...my mom could possibly die from a disease that has no cure. This is when I started to grow up, because I realized if I lost another parent, I would be in this game of life alone. All I could do was ask for prayer and try to pray myself. I continued to pray and ask God to get me out of the hole I was in. That's when I began to notice a change. I became less angry about my sister, my mother was doing better, and more blessings were coming our way. By the grace of God, my mother eventually beat cancer.

I know I never really touched on having a father figure because that didn't come until later. While growing up, I never concerned myself with wondering how the future would be with me not having a father. I was more focused on why my daddy was taken from us so soon. I blamed myself a lot because I believed if he had taken care of himself and not had to worry so much about me or others, he would've still been here.

When I was nine, a man I looked at as a father figure came into my life. I was excited that my mother was dating, but for some reason, whenever he came around, I felt different. I wasn't used to sharing my mother, who was technically my mother and my father. However, after some time passed, I felt that little void of missing my dad filling. Never did I want anyone to replace my dad, but what I did want was someone to fill the hole in my heart that was there as a result of his death. I was getting to know him, and being around him made me feel like I finally had the father figure I'd been yearning to have. He treated me like I was his daughter. I started calling him "Dad" because I felt he had earned the right to be called such. However, me referring to him as my dad caused issues with my family, mainly on my father's side. Soon, though, my family began to accept that I felt he was a father—my father figure.

In the summer of 2018, my mother lost her job, so funds got tight. My brother and I were limited on the things we could have, which neither one of us was happy about. Several months later, we had to move to a hotel for two months. When the money ran out, and we would no longer afford to stay there, we bounced around from relative to relative. Ultimately, we landed on the street and was washing up in public restrooms. In April of 2019, my mother was offered a temporary job with a company. Around June or July of the same year, we started staying with my mom's godmother. In late July of 2019, she got a call from the school where she temporarily worked, and they extended her a full-time permanent position. On October 5, 2019, we moved into a condo—a place we could finally call home. As I continue my journey of overcoming my pain, I vow to find my purpose.

Brittany is a woman on the path to being better and doing better. She has a desire to encourage others on their journey to finding their purpose. As a mother, educator, and believer of Christ, Brittany has developed a resilience that has allowed her to push through tough and trying battles—from childhood well into adulthood. It is her desire to share her story and be a beacon of hope and encouragement for others who may encounter similar battles and circumstances. Brittany's pride and joy are her two young sons, who drive her desire to end cycles of generational curses.

PLACING THE PIECES

When we speak of putting a nail in something, it implies that something is being constructed, built, fastened, or even the end of a thing. In the scope of my own life, and where I stand currently, I am doing all of these things. The pieces that were given to me all have their respective places. Now it's time to put them together to build something beautiful. What happens, though, when you have pieces but don't necessarily know how they fit together? That, my friend, is the beauty that I am learning from this life. It's the putting together of all of those pieces that makes our lives beautiful. But what are the pieces? Where are they?

They are experiences, the lessons we learn (or in the case of some, don't learn), the choices, and the company we keep. They all play a part in the life we live. We were all given one life to live—each with our purpose and destiny in tow. But sometimes, the putting together of all these pieces wears you down, injures you, and can have you ready to throw in the towel.

I can remember when I was expecting my son. While preparing for him, I focused on putting together furniture. Fortunately, they came with instructions, but I decided the instructions would slow me down. So, I put them to the side. After a few attempts to put bolts and hinges where they didn't fit, I became stressed and frustrated, realizing there was a reason for the instructions. There was no way I was going to put the crib together using my logic. I caved in and finally read the directions. A project that was taking me forever to finish was completed in minutes because I accepted the tools given to me to finish my project.

I guess I should say that I have been navigating through my life the same way I was putting the crib together, refusing to utilize the tools and the guide that life presented to me. I've had no problem identifying some of my pieces; this package came with sadness, low self-esteem, and being compared to other people and coming up short. It was certainly an area I didn't want to be in, and the sad part was I didn't know what to do about it. Unfortunately, I accepted these pieces as my identity and let them define me.

Now, let's be clear. I didn't have the perfect childhood, but I didn't have a terrible one either. My parents were divorced, but I had relationships with them both. Growing up, I didn't have a ton of friends, but my sister was my best friend, and we made memories that we still laugh about today.

I was very self-conscious about my appearance, always wondering what other people thought of me. Specifically, I wondered if I was attractive. No one had ever told me that I was beautiful. Personally, I couldn't say I was attractive or unattractive. When I looked in the mirror, I saw nothing that I would call pretty. It was easier to believe I wasn't anything special. This is where my low expectations of myself took control and fed my insecurities. The cute button-nosed girl, with long, thick, beautiful hair and big gapped-tooth smile, was ready for this great big world. Regretfully, that's not how I saw myself. I had a teacher in elementary school who made hurtful comments about me. I started believing the things she was saying about me. This interfered with my desire to learn and excel in school. It would be a lie to say that she alone was the reason I lacked confidence, but she certainly played a part in it. Some people's words and actions left me internalizing how I felt about myself and feeling like I had no place in the world.

At home, I had two households to adapt to, and neither were strangers to forms of abuse. Domestic, mental, verbal, physical, emotional, substance, sexual…it was all there, present, and accounted for. Between school, home, and church, I was having a difficult time finding a place where I fit in. Church was the one place where I could seek refuge. My mom had me active in the church. We attended every Sunday service, Bible study, youth retreat, revival, convention, convocation, and business meeting. You name it; we were there.

It was a lot, but it laid a foundation for me. Even though we spent the bulk of our time in church, I still struggled to find my niche. It should have been easier for me because kids in the church did trips together, served together, and worshipped together. So, it was definitely a place where a child could develop relationships. Sure, I knew a lot of people, but that didn't necessarily translate into friendships. When I did begin to form friendships, I found myself uncomfortable. I had spent a lot of time in my own head, being too self-conscious to initiate friendships. As an adult, I don't regret anything. If I could, I would speak to the young woman with all the insecurities. I would tell her how amazing she was and is.

After high school, I followed the typical route of going to college to continue my education. I ended up back at home just as quick as I left, due to circumstances beyond my control. I was bitter and resentful. I saw my peers graduating, starting new business ventures, traveling the world, and starting beautiful families, while I was stagnant and going nowhere. I soon found myself in a perfect storm of depression, anxiety, and low self-esteem.

My bad days outweighed my good days. I tried hard to fill the voids that I had no idea how to fix. There I was, back with pieces of myself that I had no clue what to do with. As I watched my peers living their lives, I wanted to feel just as successful and for my life to be meaningful, too. My joy was gone, and I didn't know how to get it back. I was only in my twenties, and I felt like a complete failure.

It wasn't all bad, though. While dealing with not being able to continue toward getting my degree, I kept myself busy. I found a decent job, purchased my first car, and fell in love.

These things satisfied me, but I wasn't happy. Was it the degree? Money? Who I was dating? I had no clue.

My "real" relationship lasted for about four years. Prior to this relationship, I hadn't really dated in high school. We were amazing together. He treated me good and showed me a different type of guy than the ones I was used to. It felt good finally having somebody to be comfortable with for once and to be able to let my guard down. We were young and living a life that we weren't ready for. Before I knew it, I had been in four relationships over the ten years I was out of school.

Every relationship was based on cheating, something that I wouldn't tolerate. But my choice in men was based on what I had seen as a child. Thank God, I got with a therapist who educated me on these destructive patterns. After each disastrous relationship, I walked away more broken than I went in. Next thing I knew, I was echoing my childhood, just in different ways.

I found myself tolerating and settling for things that I said I never would. I would lay on the floor crying while watching as my unfaithful boyfriends slept peacefully. I tried my hand at cheating but found that I'm not about that life. It's not who I am. Things got so bad in my dating life that I began unraveling. Two of these relationships had produced children. I had to try to be a good mother and muster up the strength to keep going for my babies. It felt like everything I touched was destined to fail, so why keep trying? My physical appearance started to reveal what had been happening on the inside. The mask I thought was covering everything had fallen away.

The issues in my last relationship had me praying more than ever. These prayers brought tears to my eyes, a bottle of alcohol in one hand, and all the pills I had in the other. I was tired of not feeling like I had a place. I was tired of failing, tired of being a single mom, and tired of feeling like sex was the only time I was noticed. I was tired of being tired.

With children who needed a roof over their heads, I put on my smiley face and got stuff done. My thoughts weren't flat out suicidal, but I was no stranger to telling myself it was okay to do what would make me feel better. I don't know what stopped me. I had already visualized my funeral in my head. If this was the way it had to be, then so be it. I was okay with whatever happened.

Eventually, panic and anxiety attacks set in, which were a bit more difficult to conceal. It also meant everything I had kept quiet was now exposed. It's difficult to hide when you have to go to the hospital. That lasted for at least two to three years. I had gotten so low that all I could do was cry and call on God.

My cardiologist sat me down before giving me a monitor to wear for two weeks and told me that his patients are typically older. At my age, I shouldn't be sufferings from the conditions I had. He told me that he knew stress when he saw it. Being in and out of doctors' offices so often was becoming exhausting. I continued to pray, but things didn't get better right away. In fact, things got worse. Bills didn't get paid, and I felt trapped. My father fell ill and ultimately passed away, and I was in a relationship I knew I needed to end.

Still, I kept praying. Despite being tired and feeling defeated, I began to study the Word more closely and get to know God for myself. That's when things started to change. Trying to fix things myself only ended up in me doing more damage. It was time for me to believe God's word and allow Him to guide me in my life. I finally ended my bad relationship. I began to lose physical weight, and it was almost as if I got a second wind. This time around, I used the directions that were given. Every single piece of me that I had no idea what to do with before, I now saw through different lenses. I realized that I wasn't the reason my exes weren't satisfied. It was because they weren't whole either.

Most importantly, everything I believed about myself— whether through insecurities, doubt, or trauma—was not true! The difference has been visible, which I didn't realize until hearing from people around me that there was "something different" about me. I will stand today and say that's a "grace glow." My identity is much GREATER now that I'm not trying to blindly put the pieces of my life together. Some pieces came with me; others I chose to remove because they were altering the way I was truly designed. Today, I recognize every piece for what it is and am grateful that they are being constructed into something bigger, better, and beautiful…and that's what I can identify with.

Charron Monaye is an adored storyteller who have evolved into a Who's Who in America's Arts and Literature. With over twenty-five years in the industry, Charron has been recognized as a literary game-changer who doesn't mind adapting words into legacies.

Her signature coaching style and personal experiences made Love the Real You: Uncovering your "WHY" & Affirming You're Enough and STOP Asking for Permission & Give Notice: How to Accept & Attain Who You Are Without Validation, Amazon Best Sellers. My Side of the Story and Get Out of your Own Way were adapted into successful stage plays that premiered in Philadelphia, Pennsylvania, Washington D.C, Hollywood, California, and Off Broadway in Times Square, New York. UnBreak My Heart: From Scorn to Finding Love Again, I Want to Quit My Job: 8 Entrepreneurial Strategies for Massive Results While Employed, Fear Is a Crime: How to Overcome Fear & Face Your Destiny, Secure Your Legacy, and When Shift Happens: 21 Days of Celebrating the Lessons of Life & Detours highly sought after book releases within the poetry, devotional, entrepreneur, and self-help genres.

Utilizing many of the same tactics commonly used today, Charron gave a new meaning to what it means to "share your truth" and exemplifies just how far your truth will take you. From her then-unprecedented writing techniques to the continuously innovative ways she uses social issues, current events, timeless messages, and her expertise as a poet, ghostwriter, scriptwriter, songwriter and storyteller, Charron remains a cutting-edge writer who pushes all boundaries.

Charron has a Bachelor of Arts in Political Science from West Chester University, a Master's in Public Administration from Keller Graduate School of Management, a Certificate in Paralegal Studies and Life Coaching, and a Doctorate of Philosophy (Humane Letters) from CICA International University & Seminary. She was also appointed as "Fellow of the Most Excellent Order of International Experts (FOIE)" in the field of Entrepreneurship from the United Nations and has been awarded and recognized for her work as an author, book publisher and playwright. She is also the Founder and CEO of Pen Legacy, LLC., and Pen Legacy Publishing.

Charron is a member of Zeta Phi Beta Sorority, Inc., Order of Eastern Star and First Baptist Church of Crestmont. She resides in Wesley Chapel, Florida, and is a proud mother of two sons, Christopher and Craig.

Contact Info:
Business Website: www.penlegacy.com
Author Website: www.charronmonaye.com
Email: info@penlegacy.com
Facebook & Twitter: PenLegacy
Instagram: iamcharronmonaye

THE GRAVEYARD IS THE RICHEST PLACE ON EARTH

If a baby boomer raised you, you were probably taught to honor the principles of work. Work, meaning a job that you clock in for eight hours and praise God daily to have so you can pay your bills. However, what "work" actually equates to is committing hours of your life in exchange for monetary compensation, and hopefully, your job allows you the opportunity to "borrow" hours to cover the time you are away from work due to an illness or a much-needed vacation. And should you have to end up caring for a family member, cross your fingers and pray that you will qualify for Family and Medical Leave, which is unpaid time. This system of work has been in place for centuries. Imagine being an ambitious kid with tons of dreams and being told, "The only thing you should be focused on is graduating from high school, getting a job, and retiring. A pension is guaranteed, whereas your dreams may never come true. So, stay focused."

Imagine having a gift or talent that is never allowed to manifest because you have to work, and quitting your job to chase a dream is unheard of and even considered a crazy notion by some people's standard. Les Brown once said, "The graveyard is the richest place on Earth." It took me years to understand that saying, but as I got older, I learned the graveyard is where you "find all the hopes and dreams that were never fulfilled, the books that were never written, the songs that were never sung, the inventions that were never shared, and the cures that were never discovered. All because someone was too afraid to take that first step, didn't keep with the problem, or lacked the determination to carry out their dream." Truly understanding this message made me decide between my gift or my job, because I have yet to find a career. I thought back to when my elementary school teacher told my mother, "Charron is going to be a writer because she is so talkative." Or the time when I recited my poem "Alone" during the United Negro College Fund Banquet at the age of twelve. Or when I wrote for the Philadelphia Association of Paralegals and received reviews, press, and acknowledgements while being a staff writer.

Being a writer is who I was; it was my therapy and how I survived. Since I was never told my gift mattered just as much as, if not more than, my income, I ignored the potential of my gift. I used it for school, writing papers for others, and correcting correspondence, but I never fully used my gift for its intended purpose. I used to tell myself, "If I'm not careful, I'm going to be one of those rich people in the graveyard." I would ask for help from my peers on how to hone my gift, but they would quote me some ridiculous price that I could not afford. I used Google to learn the how-tos, but without a physical person to walk with me, my dreams became extinct. Soon, I only focused on "working" to pay the bills and taking care of my kids. I gave up on my gift. I couldn't afford it, and no one was willing to help me. Being a mother and employee, I could not always "borrow my time" to travel to a free event in another city so I could network or gain exposure. I knew my gift was worthy enough to be seen, but nobody knew me. So, dream voided.

But, in 2008, the recession hit. I was facing a divorce, eviction, having anxiety attacks, unemployed, and being hounded by debt collectors. I had nothing and felt like nothing. I cried so much that I had no more tears left in me to shed. My boys did everything they could to cheer me up, but it only made me feel like more of a failure. Cheering me up is not something my young boys should have thought they had the responsibility to do. How could someone be doing well one day, and the next, they are so far beneath rock bottom that they would have to climb upward to reach it? I had past-due bills piling up on the table and no financial help anywhere. I had shoulders to cry on, but I needed a source of income, a new life, and a savior to get back to the right side of living.

To make matters worse, I started working for a temp agency. Every day I would sit at that job highly pissed off because here I was a woman with a bachelor's degree and certification but working eight-hour days for ten dollars an hour. My pride was shot, and if someone wanted to kill me, I would have welcomed it. You probably think I should have been grateful because I had a job at least, but it was not enough. I was barely staying afloat. However, my boys never missed a beat. I couldn't say the same for myself, though, with me missing many meals. I couldn't make them suffer for my stupidity, so I chose to suffer alone.

From that temp job, I went to work for Bell & Bell Attorney at Law as a paralegal. The pay was no better, and I went from traveling to Blue Bell to Center City, Philadelphia. Now I had the expense of gas and train fare. Things just kept getting more and more interesting, for lack of a better word. But, even with the nothingness of that job, when it came to my ego, it introduced me to entrepreneurship. During my commute on the train or while sitting at my desk at work, I would lose myself in thoughts about how great it would be to have my own business and hire others to work for me while I chill at home or escape to my beach house for the weekend. (James and Jennifer, the attorneys I worked for, did not miss a Friday at the beach.) I would start getting excited at the thought that my writing could make those things happen for me, but then, I could hear my dad's voice saying, "You better not quit that job." My mother's voice would follow with, "You have kids to think about." Then I envisioned my boys standing there looking at me sadly, which made me quickly abort the idea. For the remainder of the train ride, I would occupy myself with reading the metro newspaper.

November 23, 2008. By then, I had lost every ounce of fight I had in me. I had to go to housing court to face the consequences of not being able to pay my rent. The apartment's attorney and the judge let me have it. Not being able to afford legal representation, I had to beg for and accept assistance. Seeing my pity, the judge told the apartment's attorney to give me thirty days to come up with the back rent and court cost. COURT COST! Just kill me, please! How the hell am I going to come up with that amount of money? But, I humbly accepted the judgement and caught the train back to the place that was still my home for the time being.

Once home, I dropped to the floor and cried. I could barely pay the bills I had, and now there was a bill for over three thousand dollars that I had to pay before December 30, 2008. Just when I felt I had lost the fight, my oldest son Chris said, "Mommy, write about it." I hadn't written in years, and simply writing about it wouldn't get the money I needed for the payment. So, my boys and I would still end up homeless. But, instead of letting my son know I had just about given up, I forced a smile and replied, "Okay, baby. Mommy will." He wiped away my tears and sat on the floor with me. Then Craig walked over and sat in my lap. I looked at the composition book on the floor for a few moments before picking it up and starting to write.

The next day at work, I talked to James about my troubles, and he asked me if I had a gift that I could do very well. "I write," I told him, and he replied, "Then you're not broke." That day, I cried on his desk, frustrated because I didn't feel like I was capable of using my gift of writing to be successful.

I was a single mom with two boys who depended on me for everything, and I had to work so that I could get a pension once I retired. I could not sacrifice anymore. James looked me, and with a strong voice, he said, "You can't let your gift die. Something in you must live for your children. Why make them suffer because of what you've been told? Some people work all their lives and don't live long enough to get their pension or social security. You must be whole and available to be their mother. You are very important."

Even though I had heard him, what I knew about chasing dreams came to the forefront and dismissed everything he said. It wasn't until a producer out of Atlanta replied to one of my poems on Facebook that things started to turn around. I felt like my dreams were within reach. He liked my poetry and asked if I wrote songs. I replied, and he sent three tracks for me to write the lyrics. Wait! What is going on? I lived in Philadelphia, and he was in Atlanta. I wondered what he saw in me that people in Philly or others who I knew didn't.

I received the tracks, had my sorority sister, Summer, reference them, and then sent them back. He loved them so much that he sent me more tracks and used my songs for his artists. It was amazing to hear artists singing my lyrics on commercial albums. Is this happening? I was finally utilizing my gift and living a dream. From that opportunity came a book deal, and I adapted that book into a stage play that I co-produced. I traveled to DC to showcase my play in the theater festival and created a publishing company through which I published other people's books and my own. I also formed and trademarked my business, Pen Legacy®, and became a coach. In 2018, I premiered my play Get Out of Your Own Way in Hollywood, California, and I accomplished all this while employed but now with the Federal Government.

When I realized I could "work" and be an entrepreneur at the same time, the limitations that I once knew lifted. I no longer kept my gifts in bondage, and I stopped quitting on myself because of what I was raised to believe. Even though I sometimes work harder because I am an employee and entrepreneur, the rewards and blessings come in abundance, and those things that once worried me are distant memories. I will never forget the year 2008 because it made me realize I need my gift to survive. I need the blessings that it brings to thrive. I need the therapy that writing provides, which lets me live with anxiety without any issues. This gift has many purposes, and now that I am utilizing it, life for me has gotten so much better. God is smiling down on me. The "right" people know me, many people want to learn from me, and others enjoy working with me. My bills are paid, my credit is great, and my kids are flourishing. Most importantly, my boys and I are rich on earth and living in our wealth. It gets no better than that.

If you are living life with untapped dreams or goals, use my story as motivation. Sometimes I wonder what my life would be like now if I hadn't waited so long to use my gifts blessed upon me. I remember being in Schmidt Hall on West Chester University campus, and my boyfriend Hasan used to tell me, "You are such a great writer." Even back then, I used to smile at his compliment but ignore him at the same time. I never imagined my writing could bring me to where I am now or make what was once impossible possible. I had many people who believed in me, but when certain ideals, principles, and rules are instilled in a person, it is hard for them to see the options available to them during their journey. So, remember this. Even if you are working a job, you can still manifest your dreams. I know tons of people working a nine-to-five but living out their dream by utilizing their gifts or passions. With the pressures of the day-to-day hustle of life, wouldn't it feel good to be able to do something you enjoy and possibly get paid for doing it? Wouldn't you feel that much more inspired or worthy of life if you were living to enjoy it instead of only living to work and eventually die?

The graveyard is the richest place on Earth, but it doesn't have to be. Use my testimony to motivate you, and if you need my coaching services to help you tap in so you can enjoy your gifts on this side of Earth, then I can help you with that. Trust me, doing so will be far more rewarding, fulfilling, and legendary for you and your family than you sitting on your dreams. The greatest reward I received after tapping into my gift is knowing that my children now have a business that they can collect on, work for, and operate for the rest of their lives. Even after I depart from this earth, they will continue to receive royalties from everything my name is on that is sold or purchased. My businesses are now inheritances that will carry them and the next generations to come. It feels good to know I will be able to leave them with a successful business rather than draining debt. So, even though I was taught to work for a pension, being an entrepreneur has allowed me to create something that will outlive me here on earth and continue to sustain others even when I am in the graveyard.

Debaro Wilson Robinson is a native of Washington, DC and the proud mother of two world changers Kiawana Leaf and Juan Butler. Along parenting the two, she also adores her only granddaughter Azariah Leaf. A few of Debaro passions includes shopping, traveling, quality time, eating crabs with family, and worshiping God!

Debaro attended DC Public Schools where she is a proud graduate of Theodore Roosevelt High School, in Washington, Dc.! She attended Norfolk State University majoring in Early

Childhood Education and later attended Strayer University majoring in Business Administration. Debaro is a born-again Christian, devoted wife, member of Greater Mount Calvary Holy Church for over 40 years, and she's excited to share her journey with you how she has put a nail, ending her walk of fear!

WALKING OUT OF FEAR

Oh, magnify the Lord with me. Let us rejoice and be glad in it. I do not know where to start, but God has indeed been on my side. I had my strongholds, but He has allowed me to trust in Him and overcome them living by faith and walking out of fear.

My battle began in 2016. Wow, it has been four years that I have been battling my spiritual awakening and not living to my full potential that God has called me to be.

Well, let me get this journey started. The year of 2016 was very rough and stressful and for me. I had a supervisor that micromanaged everything I did. I t seemed as if everything that I did was not good enough for her. What seems to amaze me is that I would always receive a good evaluation from her. I recall one day, she gave me an assignment to complete, which I did, but it was not to her satisfaction. So, she decided to write me up. I continued to do what was required, but what felt as harassment never stopped.

2016 my health also began to decline. My husband and I were preparing for our summer vacation to Jamaica. When I went to my niece's so she could style my hair in braids, she discovered a bald spot. I had no clue what it was, so I thought no more of it. As the months went by, I noticed my hair shedding in patches when I would comb it. Growing concerned, I went to my daughter, who is a cosmetologist, and had her look at my scalp. After inspecting the bald spots, she said, "Ma, you have alopecia." Having never heard of the condition before, I began to cry and immediately started praying to God. Even though I worried about what could be causing my hair loss, I continued to embrace my faith and rely on God.

I visited a dermatologist to evaluate my hair, and the diagnosis was indeed alopecia areata, which affects the immune system. I followed up with my general practitioner to discuss my new diagnosis, test my thyroid, and tested for lupus. The test results were negative, "Thank God", but I discovered that one of the side effects of my high blood pressure medication was hair loss. My physician prescribed a new prescription, and I began getting steroid shots in my scalp for the alopecia. For months, I went through the process of receiving those shots, but there was no change. As painful and stressful this process became. Through it all, I continued to walk in faith than my fears.

During this time, my supervisor was asked to resign. With my hair still shedding, I felt some sort of relief and peace from my workplace. I was introduced to a stylist named Keith Harley, who specializes in Trichology. I contacted Mr. Harley, explaining my hair situation and he recommended that I purchase his therapeutic kit. I still use his products today.

From my supervisor's resignation, I had no more bald spots. Believing the stress, anxiety, and tension from my workplace was the cause of my alopecia cause more so the medication. I encourage women who have developed alopecia of any form from any cause to contact Mr. Harley. His products are wonderful and does wonders!

2017, new year and new beginnings, I thought the year would be for me. However, I found myself back in the familiar situation with a new supervisor that was unapproachable, inaccessible, and distant. I worked in a hospital where rumors had been spreading that the hospital would be closing soon. Weeks if not months had passed before my supervisor eventually started communicating with us, assuring that the rumors were indeed true.

On October 7, 2017, I remember that day so vividly! I was called into my director's office and informed that the Denial and Appeals Department was closing. This department was the department that I worked under and I was informed that that day would be my last day of employment. I cannot begin to tell you how shocked, broken, and frustrated that I instantly became to hear that I had lost my job. The director apologized profusely and offered to assist me in any way they could to help with my job search.

With no idea of how I was going to maintain, pay my bills,

support my family, yet alone live a life, I sobbed tears of worry and defeat. Every thought and question went through my head in the matter of seconds. "What about my healthcare? What about everyday life? What about this, what about that?" How was I to maintain? The thought instantly troubled me! However, I did receive a ten-week severance package, which lasted through the end of the year. As well, I also had one hundred hours of PTO that carried me to the middle of January. Startling myself, all alone God already had a plan for me!

I instantly applied for unemployment but was told to reapply after my severance would end. Then I applied online for COBRA, which was so expensive I could not afford. However, with all my pre-existing conditions, I could not afford to have it. So, I called the insurance office to inquire about how COBRA works, and the representative informed me that my plan was paid in full until December 31, 2018. God is so faithful! I did not have to use any of my funds to pay for health or dental insurance. But what about once the funds ended? As for my retirement plan, I had one but did not want to use it because, as it states, it is a plan for RETIREMENT. After going back and forth, worrying myself. I put a nail, ending my walk of fear into my walk of faith. Not understanding then, I had to trust in the Lord and lean not on my own understanding. (Proverbs 3:5)

After receiving that revelation, I decided to withdraw the funds and take care of all my financial obligations. No one ever knew that I was unemployed. I did not wear my worry on my face or allow it to consume me. Because I released how blessed and fortunate that I still was despite being unemployed. I had food on the table, clothes on my back, a roof over my head, but most importantly a peace of mind. Although my retirement funds were used for my financial obligations, I decided to trust God and stop walking in fear.

If I could title the year of 2018, I would call it Surgery Pains to Blessings. While out of work for a year, I wanted to do something for myself. I was scheduled to have an abdominoplasty on May 9, 2018, right before my trip to Aruba in July. A $600 non-refundable deposit was due to begin the pre-op process. I provided my payment, and the process began. While going through the pre-op process, my blood pressure was unusually higher than normal. Concerned, I canceled the surgery but forgot that the deposit was non-refundable. I met with the office manager to see what options I had to cancel and receive the deposit. Of course, I was told I would be okay, and the only option that I had was to reschedule or count the $600 deposit a loss.

The surgery went as scheduled, and everything went well. During my first post-op appointment, everything looked great. I was excited to fully recover and embrace something I have wanted to do for me! However, the following week, I had another good appointment, except I was informed that my oxygen level was a little low. The surgeon did not seem to be too concerned about it, though he seen my concerns, stating it would increase. The next follow-up appointment took place two weeks later. That was when my tubes were removed. Everything looked well, but my oxygen level the same, a little low. During my fourth appointment, my oxygen level was lower than it had been during my previous appointments. The doctor immediately sent me to the emergency room from his office so I could have a CAT scan. When the result came back, it showed I had a small blood clot on my left lung. As I cried, I questioned God, Why me? Suddenly, the scripture Isaiah 53:5 came to my spirit: "But he was wounded for our transgressions, he was bruised for our iniquities: the chastisement of our peace was upon him; and with his stripes we are healed." With those words, I continued to walk out of fear, knowing that God would heal me!

After receiving a blood thinner shot, I was discharged to go home. God began to minister to me that my body had been traumatized, I must trust in Him and believe that "no weapon formed against me shall prosper" (Isaiah 54:17). I was placed on a blood thinner Xarelto for six months to help prevent developing more clots and having a stroke. Also, to prevent this from happening, I began walking multiple times a day to build up my oxygen level.

My trip to Jamaica was amazing, to be able to get away, and relax for a little while. But I wanted to do something more for myself. So, having always desired to be a teacher, I enrolled in the CDA (Child Development Associate) program at UDC (University of the District of Columbia). It was a great class, so encouraging, and inspiring. After completing and passing the course, I had to volunteer a certain number of hours working with children. Since I was not working, I applied to a temp agency. The pay was not very much, but I was grateful for the opportunity since I had no job.

In October, I received a call from the University of Maryland Capital Region Health Hospital for an Accounts Receivable position. The interview went well, but I did not get the job because I lacked the experience. However, something good did come out of the interview. The interviewer was so impressed with my professionalism that she recommended me to one of her co-partners in another department. The next day, I received a call from the Case Management Department to set up an interview for a position that was being created in that very moment. Talk about God opening and orchestrating doors for me! All that I had to do was trust in Him and lean not on my own understanding (Proverbs 3:5).

My first day of employment with the University of Maryland Capital Region Health Hospital was December 10, 2018, just before the year ended as well as my COBRA plan. Valuing my life lessons of ending my walk out of fear into my faith.

I never thought family and friends would be the ones to betray me. That is a painful experience. I am a caring, trustworthy, dependable, lovable, reserved, sensitive, strong person, but I do not like foolishness. I know I am not for everyone and became comfortable in understanding that that is okay.

In my relationships in 2019, I felt most attacked by the ones I valued so much. I had a loss of trust. I value the definition of friendship and family to the extreme. I think of other's feelings before acting and thinking of myself. I did not realize the depth of my pain until I had to defend myself, releasing my truths, not knowing God was preparing me for my purpose.

I was in a trial to learn how to resist the urge to fight. I had to become at ease to be quiet, stop explaining myself to make others comfortable while belittling myself in agreeance with them to later harm me only. I had to learn and understand to ask the Lord to forgive them, for they know not what they do (Luke 23:34) even when I did not fully understand myself. I cried and cried from the harsh realities of betrayal. I wanted nothing more than to maintain friendships that I had built. But I did not know it at the time, God was strengthening my heart for a purpose and a divine impact. What I felt was betrayal in many situations and believed what mattered the most. I understood the "betrayal" was my discomfort to stagnation. This season was showing me that I had outgrown a lot of relationships. God was and still is preparing me for something big, that I would trust my walk out of fear of losing and valuing friends that prevents me from growing.

I remember believing that I was really in my awakening, not ignoring anymore signs, to fully commit to living my life in faith than fear. A storm came, and the wind blew so hard that suddenly, I heard a loud snap! As I was leaving my parents home, unlocking my car doors, moments away from my granddaughter and I approaching the car to get in. A utility pole fell right on my car! The roof had collapsed, front window was cracked, back window had shattered, glass was everywhere, and the driver's door was damaged. Becoming so numb this fright turned into anger thinking, "how would I get to and from work and how much would the repairs be"?

Not really realizing it was God's protection over me, taking away the anger so that I could focus more on him. God is closer than any brother. (Proverbs 18:24)

When I think of the goodness of Jesus and all that he has done for me, my soul cries out HALLELUJAH! I thank God for saving me. (Psalms 18:1-3)

On March 17, 2020, I tested positive for the coronavirus. I panicked and asked God why me, and I heard him say, "Why not you? I am building your faith to move you to the next level of your life. People know I am a healer, but I need you to know for yourself and end your walk of fear with Me.

He reminded me that he healed me from areata alopecia in 2016, which today, I don't have any more bald spots. He sustained me when I was unemployed in 2017, and I lacked for nothing. He healed me from a blood clot in my left lung in 2018, which is no longer in existence. He strengthened me from my feelings of betrayed and protected me from a storm in 2019.

"So why do you have such little faith Debaro?" God asked me. "I am the same God yesterday, today, and forevermore. I let you live and not die. You are my servant to fulfill every purpose I promise you and sowing unexpected heights. No weapon formed against you shall prosper. The power of your faith is greater than the voice of fear. You are covered by my blood and that it is clear to the enemy."

During my time of being quarantined, I did a lot of soul-searching, reading, worshipping, and praying. God told me it was time for me to reset, reconnect, and revive. I must give God my weakness, so he can give me His strength to face this challenge head-on.

It was exceedingly difficult to cope with COVID-19. Watching news reports about how this disease was killing thousands of people a day and how there was a shortage of ventilators was frightening. It left me wondering would there be a ventilator available for me should I need it. Most days, I was left in tears because there were so many unanswered questions about this deadly disease. I had to remember I was still alive, and that was by the grace of God, He had spared me yet again. For that, I am humbly grateful. I will forever praise Him for His goodness.

I had been quarantined for twenty-four days, and I was finally released by the CDC from isolation on April 9, 2020. I was excited about seeing my family. I am sure you may be wondering why I had to be quarantined for so long. Well, I had numerous symptoms of the COVID-19 virus that were hard to get under control, and I needed to be monitored consistently.

On April 10, 2020, I was retested to be cleared to go back to work. My anxiety was through the roof because some of my co-workers had tested positive, an employee had died, and ninety patients had also tested positive. So, I was in no hurry to go back to work. God had to remind me to trust in Him and lean not on my own understanding.

On Monday, April 13, 2020, I received a call from my physician. I had tested positive once again. I was devastated. I thought that nightmare was behind me. How could this be happening again? I began to question God's word, and yet again, He reminded me that I was covered in His blood.

I went into quarantine again, and on April 17, 2020, I was given the rapid test, which came back negative. I was also given the lab test on Monday, April 20, 2020, and that was negative, as well.

Our God can do all things exceedingly and abundantly above all. Still, during this pandemic, I now know that Jesus was always there, and holding true to His word, He never left me in this 4-year window of life calamities. He is my Jehovah Rapha, my HEALER and I encourage you to put a nail, ending your walk of fear!

Life can be brutal, unforgiving, and beautiful, all at the same time. For *Kiawana "Key" Leaf,* she has experienced this and a whole lot more. A God-made entrepreneur, author, actress, and inspirational speaker, Kiawana aspires to inspire, empower, and embrace millennials across the nation. Through her first business venture, Empower Too Inspire, LLC, Kiawana helps women who are survivors of domestic abuse and assists those who have experienced traumatic events to find and fulfill their life purpose. The foundation of

Empower Too Inspire is built on women's empowerment and kingdom advancement.

Kiawana is a rising star who was featured on TV One's "For My Man", WUSA9, and Ari Squires' soul-stirring documentary "No More Chains 2". While life has thrown many obstacles her way, Kiawana's faith in God has never wavered. She dedicated her life to Jesus Christ at the age of twelve. Kiawana's greatest inspiration comes from her greatest joy—her daughter, Azariah. Kiawana looks forward to being an inspiration to many who are seeking healing and spiritual growth. It is her dream, vision, purpose, and power to Empower Too Inspire!

Contact Info:
Business Website: www.empowertooinspire.org
Author Website: www.kiawanaleaf.com
Email: empowertooinspire@gmail.com
Facebook: Kiawana Leaf
Instagram: Kiawana___ & Empowertooinspire

EMBRACING MY EMBARRASSMENT

Traumatic experiences, one after another. I was most comfortable suffocating in what felt like an embarrassment to me. Ashamed, guilty, and insecure. I felt those emotions and more. I suffered in silence, which was not the best thing for me. I was too embarrassed to embrace what was happening to me. I did not want to speak of what possibly could happen to me. I realized how I continued to run in my repetitive cycle full of toxic traits.

My name is Kiawana, better known as Key. Best-selling author, actress, entrepreneur, and founder of Empower Too Inspire, LLC. Raised by an absentee father, I was a domestic violence survivor who later turned into the abuser. I filled voids with alcohol, drugs, and sexual addictions to satisfy my unhealthy cravings. I began to backslide, blurring my vision of faith and trust in Him. I believed God had forgotten all about me. So many calamities were happening to me that I began wearing a mask that portrayed false strength, happiness, self-love, and purpose. I did not know my true identity. My most embarrassing moments helped to define me. What I believed were my weakest moments turned my pain into the jumpstart I needed to get my momentum going again. I am most proud of Key.

You see, I dared not tell the world that my father was not present in my life as I desired him to be. I dared not tell the world that I was a domestic violence victim for three years, where one quick bullet almost changed my whole life. I dared not share my story of how circumstances turned the tables, and I became the abuser. My self-esteem was so low that I believed I needed a significant other to have sex. I needed that person to shower me with attention; it was the attention that made me feel beautiful and pretty. I secretly admired the video vixens, wondering why the same career was not in my future. I was overwhelmed, depressed, stressed, lost, and broken. Smoking and drinking were the best way for me to escape my pain. I wonder where Key would be if I did not go through this "embarrassment".

My journey of healing has been difficult—a heavy burden to carry. I was falling into a deep depression with no escape plan. I watched as the people I loved and who I thought loved me turned their backs on me. This journey I am currently on, I do not wear a façade mask. It is #MaskOffSeason, and I am not settling for anything other than being beautifully free. I quickly discovered being free will make people resent you simply because you are not where they think you should be, keeping them comfortable while you are at the weakest point in your life. Let me tell you, keep healing, growing, glowing, and evolving anyway!

It sounds easy, but this is where you apply pressure and desperately seek God, no matter what. When you feel ashamed of seeking and spreading your truth, story, and the gospel, go harder! I felt embarrassed about releasing my best-selling novel Confidence Unlocked in 2019 because I was releasing my absolute truth. I didn't want the world to know the hidden pain that had defined me. I had hidden the authentic me, and once it was out there, I couldn't take it back. Behind my glorious mask was a fraud. What I had to understand about my journey was there would be no healing if I didn't give a testimony about what I had been through. I finally understand the purpose of pain, and I am excited to help inspire others to turn their pain into power.

Can you imagine walking into the four walls of a church and boldly sharing a story like mine? All of my sins, guilt, and defeat. Can you imagine the number of side-eyes, judgement, and critics that I would receive? Those were the biggest reasons that held me back and made me continue to live my life in fear and what I believed to be most comfortable for me. If you do not take away anything else, take away this one thing from Key. NEVER seek validation or approval from any man but God! He is the only one who will truly get you through. Of course, you will have support from others, but the strength will not come from anyone other than Him.

I'm not embarrassed anymore by my testimony. I embrace

every bit of my journey. Forgive yourself before forgiving anyone else. Your peace and acceptance will first begin by forgiving and loving yourself. Being able to do so, I am able to celebrate the young lady I was and have blossomed into the God-ordained woman I am today. I put away my childish mentality and matured into my identity in Him. I stopped wanting acceptance and approval from people and only craved to make God most proud of me. I am no longer a people pleaser but addicted to completing assignments that are pleasing to Him.

No, I am not going to lie and say it doesn't hurt or that it's easy to do. I will always be one to spread the truth. I had to remove myself from some friends, family members, and even relationships that were not challenging or stretching me into who I was destined to be. People I believed would be with me forever ended up being the ones who truly hurt me. I had to end a lot of relations because I would get too comfortable, and the complacency became an uncomfortable feeling for me. I knew what I wanted and identified my ultimate goals that I was determined to reach. Not all of them were toxic or ill to my life. But they weren't ordained to progress any further in my life. Some were a distraction and not enough to keep me going. Remember, people are in your life for a reason or a season.

When I use the word "win", I don't just mean a financial win. I am speaking of mentally, emotionally, but most importantly, a spiritual win. I am certain we all can attest that 2020 is taking us on one hell of a ride. With Kobe Bryant's tragic death, many celebrities passing, the pandemic, many loved ones passing and being unable to attend their funerals, police brutality, racism, injustice, witnessing and hearing about violence, and being ignored and silenced. We all have faced traumatic experiences in 2020. Wouldn't you agree?

But, can I share something with you to encourage you through? I understand and can relate to your anger, frustration, and pain. May 2020 was the absolute worst month I've ever experienced. From grieving my childhood friend and sister transitioning in 2017, suffering approximately six loved ones passing, having to stream our matriarch's funeral service, my mother and I testing positive for COVID-19, and receiving a layoff letter. I could've lost my mind completely! In the past, I have been quick to return to my old comfort zone, but no more. I quickly evaluated myself. I had to adjust my way of thinking. Once we feel weak and can't carry on, that's when the enemy will attack. That's when we're most vulnerable and gullible to fall into Satan's traps.

I am not telling you not to feel a certain way or to ignore what is going on. But there is no way to be healed without being heard. I promise you this is not the end. Posture yourselves, embrace our turbulent times, and get ready. Don't miss His mark, and don't miss His message in all of this! There is a great and mighty cloud coming soon!

Matthew 24:29-30 tells us, "Immediately after the tribulations of those days: 'The sun will be darkened, and the moon will not give its light; the stars will fall from the sky, and the powers of the heavens will be shaken.' At that time the sign of the Son of Man (coming in His glory) will appear in heaven, and all the tribes of the earth (and especially Israel) will mourn (regretting their rebellion and rejection of the Messiah). They will see the Son of Man coming on the clouds of heaven, with power and great glory (in brilliance and splendor)."

Rid your fear and get out of your comfort zone. There is no purpose nor power there! I didn't anticipate doing a chapter in Put a Nail End It, but I realized that my plans are not His plans. When He says to move, it's best to do just that. I want to share a prayer that I released in my sophomore book release Beautifying Sins, and I pray it richly blesses, inspires, and encourages you.

Dear Father God,

You are an amazing, omnipotent, gracious, most powerful, and righteous God. You are perfect in all of Your ways. You make no mistakes nor lead any of us the wrong way. And for that, Father God, I say thank You. I thank You in advance for the way You will show Your face upon Your children. Many souls will cry out to You for deliverance and repentance. I thank you for not letting any of us go when we deserved to be released. I thank You for still loving us even when we were hurt by love.

I thank You for not judging us and looking beyond our faults and flaws even when we deserve to be condemned. Now, God, I stand in the gap for my fellow brothers and sisters. Help them to look in the mirror and see themselves the way You see them. Let them know that you are doing a new thing in their lives and here on Earth. Mend every shattered piece to see perfection as You see in us.

Allow them to pay attention and not miss your presence, oh Father God. I pray now, God, as a sign of surrendering. Forgive us, oh God, for our sinful ways. Forgive us, oh God, for our lustful thoughts. Oh God, forgive us for our brokenness and bitterness. Forgive us, God, for coping through turbulence instead of changing in the midst of it. Forgive us for putting the world before You instead of putting the world behind You. Forgive us for holding onto grudges, past pain, hurt, and abuse.

Now, God, I lift every family member in prayer. Oh God, break generational chains. God, break generational curses. Father, break the cycle and allow them to end with me. I don't want to be like them, oh God. I desire to be different; my heart thirsts to be different; I hunger to be different. Do Your works through me, oh God, and send me to Your land that the world will humble themselves and pray and seek Your face, oh God. I pray that the world sees me and believes in You. Oh God, I pray that they see how You made right my wrongs for your glory, Father God. Let Your children understand that there is a purpose in our pain, Father God, and there is a reason for every season.

Fix my mirror that the world would see You through me. Fix our lenses that our hearts would rely on You. Fix my mirror to know and understand my true identity, as You have called me to be. Father God, guide us to acknowledge our weakness. Help us to embrace our weakness and wash us clean from all of our childish things. Help us to walk in pure maturity to see Your face, oh God.

71

Now, Lord Jesus, I take a moment to admit that I am a sinner, and, Father, I ask for Your forgiveness. I believe You died on the cross for my sins and rose from the dead. Today, I turn away from childish, sinful things, and I invite You to take over my heart and my life. Purify me, oh God. Cleanse me, oh God. Have Your will and Your way. I want to trust and follow You as my Lord and Savior. I am guilty of my sins, but because I have been cleansed and I am committed and dedicated to You, that's what makes me beautiful. Not only am I guilty and have been cleansed, but I am dedicated and committed to change, grow, and evolve. I am committed to grow, glow, and evolve into who You say that I am.

Thank You for Your grace and mercy and for showing Your face to me. I'm not perfect, and I make mistakes, but that's why I need your strength, Father God, to carry me through. In my immature moments, God, give me the wisdom and discernment that I need from You. I declare and decree from this day forward our broken pieces are Your masterpiece. It is so. The only reason I'm here today is because you love me. I honor You. I am thankful. I am grateful, and I will glorify Your name forever! Even when my days get hard and life does not make sense, I know that You have a plan and purpose destined for me. So, I'm committed to growing, glowing, and evolving in You.

Love always,

A little sinner like me!

Edana J. Perry is a wife, mother, minister, and poet who is passionate about couples and families. She is always humbled to serve as a conference speaker, imparting nuggets of knowledge gained from her professional and marital journey with transparency, honesty, and humor. Reading a mystery novel while listening to gospel, jazz, and R&B is what Edana enjoys doing in her free time. Life is more than what we do!

Edana is a Pittsburgh, PA. homegirl and the youngest of three girls born to the late Charlotte Kay Johnson. After attaining a Bachelor's degree from Howard University and becoming a member of Delta Sigma Theta Sorority, Inc., Edana obtained her Master's degree in Health Services Administration from

The George Washington University. She has enjoyed a successful career in Healthcare administration for over 25 years. Life is more than what we do!

Edana has been married to Bernard Perry for 35 years. Through their celebratory and challenging moments, their joint testimony has become "yet, we will trust God". To their union, God sent three children, Taelor Necolle, Christian Bernard, and Kayla Ross, who received her angel wings on July 6, 2017. They are also proud grandparents to Ariyah and Amahri. Life is more than what we do!

Journaling and writing poetry have become pivotal to Edana's healing since the transition of Kayla. In response to losing Kayla, Edana and Bernard co-founded the Kayla Ross Perry Memorial Foundation (KRPMF) in 2019. She serves as the president of the KRPMF, whose mission is to raise awareness about epilepsy, provide scholarships, and sponsor creative arts events.

www.kaylarossperrymemorialfoundation.org

Her relationship with God and her faith gives Edana the tenacity and strength to embrace life so she will forever be #KaylaStrong.

CONFESSIONS FROM A BROKEN PLACE

I can remember when each of our three children was born to me and my husband, Bernard. Taelor Necolle, our first child, was born in 1983, followed by Christian Bernard in 1987. Bringing up the rear, our youngest, Kayla Ross, was born in 1991. Emotions were high with all of the anticipation, expectation, and apprehension associated with being parents. The unique joy each child brought to our lives is indescribable, and each child's miraculous entry into the world changed me. I was not the same woman nor the same mom after each birth. With each new addition to the family, our lives changed. Our home changed, as well. The household made adjustments as it grew to become a family of five. We felt the changes from the increase in our clothing budget and monthly grocery bill. With each addition, a new experience and dynamic emerged within our family. From tumbling classes to children's choir practice to karate class to track and soccer, our lives were full.

As I think back on that season of my life, I know I am blessed to be the mother of three unique individuals. However, I was naïve to think all three of my children would grow old with me. At age 11, our youngest Kayla was diagnosed with Juvenile Myoclonic Epilepsy (JME). Lack of sleep triggered her JME. With this diagnosis, our family experienced another shift to accommodate this new normal.

The entire family adjusted to her diagnosis by developing a keener sense of hearing so we could quickly respond when Kayla experienced a seizure or a fall. We also made sure she went to bed on time and often checked in on her once she was sleep. During her school years, we adjusted our schedules so Kayla wouldn't be left home alone. Our family adapted to our lifestyle without whining or complaining because that is what family does.

My husband and I had faith that God would one day heal Kayla. In the meantime, we were determined that Kayla would lead a "normal" life. Yes, that meant there were days when she was not pleased with our decisions concerning her bedtime, restriction of social activities, etc. It also meant there were days when we were not happy with Kayla's actions or decisions that may have been contrary to what we suggested.

With all the challenges associated with epilepsy, Kayla endured. God enabled her to experience and accomplish many great things. Yet, with the diagnosis of JME, our family lived with the reality that Kayla could have a seizure, fall, hit her head, and possibly die. Because of our faith, we did not allow our fears to prevent Kayla from living her life (most of the time). Kayla sang with the Washington Performing Arts Children of the Gospel (COTG) community choir for about 10 years. She attended Girl Scout camps and traveled to various cities with our church youth group. She was even able to go with the family to South Africa. While attending Morgan State University, she sang as a member of the University Choir, traveling around the country. She later graduated from Montgomery College. Despite the JME, we still thought our family of five would remain intact forever. But, that was not in the plan. I had no idea our family would soon be altered forever.

July 6th, 2017, began as any typical Thursday workday. I showered, dressed, and peeked in Kayla's room to ensure she was breathing okay while sleeping. By now, this had become part of our routine. However, this was not a typical workday because it was our 32nd wedding anniversary.

My husband picked me up from work a little early, and we headed to nearby Columbia, Maryland, to have dinner with my sister, my nephew, his wife, and her sister. We enjoyed dinner and great conversation. Around 7:00 p.m., I texted Kayla (as I would always do when we were out). Because she had experienced some tremors at work, Kayla was at home resting, but she did not respond to my text. Although concerned, I was not alarmed because when she did not feel well, she often slept hard.

We arrived back at our home around 10:00 p.m. As we always did after being out, we immediately headed upstairs to see about Kayla. I went to check on Kayla, while her father changed his clothes in our bedroom. I approached her room, and when I peeked in, I noticed she was face down on her pillow. Knowing something was wrong, my motherly instinct kicked in, and I fully entered her room, walking to the bed. I called her name, sitting on the bed. I put my hand on her forehead, and she was warm. But when I tried to turn her over, she was like a brick. Becoming upset, I screamed for her father.

I called her name repeatedly. "Kayla, baby, wake up!" Kayla was unresponsive to my calls. I screamed for my husband again. This time, he heard me and ran to Kayla's room to help me try to roll her over. Together, he and I managed to roll her heavy body over onto her back. Chris arrived home right then, and my husband yelled for him to come upstairs immediately. When Chris ran up the steps, he saw his father and me trying to move his sister, and he lost it. Bernard and managed to move Kayla to the floor. Bernard called 911. The operator stayed on the call while guiding us in performing CPR on our daughter.

While waiting for the ambulance to come, my husband and I took turns administering CPR on Kayla. While one of us performed CPR, the other prayed, screamed for Jesus, and cried out loud. We kept this up until the paramedics arrived.

After what seemed like a lifetime but was only about twenty minutes, the paramedics arrived. They quickly came up the stairs to Kayla's room and attached a machine to her to check her vitals. After a few minutes, one of the paramedics said "I'm sorry, ma'am. She's gone." I can remember hearing those words in disbelief. I felt like I was having an out-of-body experience. This is not happening! No! My daughter is not dead. Not my daughter.

She passed away from Sudden Unexpected Death in Epilepsy or SUDEP. Just like that, our youngest daughter was gone.

We lost our loved one suddenly, and our household was forced to make adjustments unexpectedly. What took years to build changed in a moment. Our family of five was not only interrupted but altered forever. The next several months were a blur.

For months, I was in a state of shock. The pain I felt from losing our daughter was so consuming that I did not want to live. I felt like I had been punched in the stomach and the wind knocked out of me forever. It was as if a piece of my heart had literally been ripped away. I was shocked and angry at God. Why would He allow this to happen to me, to us, to our family? I was deeply hurt.

The feeling of wanting to evaporate into the air, or disappear in the walls, or just go away plagued me. How can I, as a mother, be here without one of my children? There is something unnatural about that. How can I be present in this world without Kayla?

Her unexpected passing made it hard to visit places she and I would go together. For example, I refused to visit our favorite nail salon for two reasons. I did not want the nail technicians to ask, "Where is your daughter?" I could not bring myself to say, "My daughter passed away." The second reason I did not visit is because to be in that place reminded me too much of Kayla and that hurt.

Those months immediately following her transition, it was hard for me to be at home. I dreaded returning to our home of twenty-two years. Every day I walked into our house, I expected to see Kayla and hear her voice. But she was not there. She would never be there again. Every day I became depressed when I opened the door, and there was no Kayla. She was not with a friend; she was not at work. Our Kayla was gone and not coming back. As soon as I realized that her returning to us was not a possibility, I slipped deeper into depression. It was too much. It hurt. It was hard to sleep. It was difficult to relax. In many ways, I feel like my mind was trying to protect me by keeping me awake, because there were times I expected Kayla to come walking through the door. I could not rest. We often fell asleep around one or two o'clock in the morning because we thought if we stayed up, Kayla would come home.

Day after day, when I returned home, I expected to see Kayla. My expectation turned into disappointment. Our home was most definitely a trigger for me. Finally, I could not take it anymore and asked my husband could we sell the house. I could not bear living in that house without Kayla. So, we sold the house in December 2017. Yes, I was hurt and hurting.

When I look back on that time, I kept a journal to chronicle my experience. The first ten days after Kayla's transition, I operated on pure adrenaline. Those days were filled with announcements, family, friends, and decision-making for her celebration of life. I was literally going through the motions. All I wrote about was how much I missed Kayla. I created poems on missing her and how much this hurt, acknowledging sleepless nights and relocating our sleep area to the couch in the family room. I documented how I wept so much that my body ached. I wrote down scripture verses that aligned with my pain, hurt, and disillusionment.

As I look back through my journal, somewhere around Day 23, I wrote, "Good morning, Kayla. I woke up!" Then on Day 31, I wrote, "Good morning, Kayla. I got up today!" What I realize now is I felt like giving up back then. Yes, at times, I wanted to join Kayla. I almost gave up, but now I was choosing to get up. Despite the deep, deep pain I was experiencing, I chose to wake up and try it again. For the next thirty days or so, I was intentional in documenting that I woke up! My confession, I woke up hurt but hopeful. I must be honest here. I was not fully aware that I was exhibiting any hope because my pain was driving my life. Hence, the new reality of living in this dichotomy of hurting yet hopeful was where I found myself.

From July 2017 until about July 2019, I functioned in a fog of shock, numbness, and disbelief. I did not even realize I was in this fog until I came out of it. I was present, but not really. I was functioning by habit but not really engaged. A part of me died when Kayla died. While I was present, the Edana people knew was not. My transformation from complete fogginess to clarity, awareness, and engagement was and still is a process.

Yes, I was hurt and hurting, but something deep down in my

soul protected me and covered me. Something deep down was keeping me since I did not want to be kept. That something deep down inside of me was the love of God. Even though I was hurt and hurting, God was rebuilding me and healing me with grace, mercy, and hope. God loved me from the inside out.

My process of learning to live after death is not finished. I sought assistance and support in a variety of ways to navigate my healing journey from grief.

Within a month (August 2017) after our daughter's transition, we began grief counseling to help me and Bernard deal with our emotions and the reality of losing Kayla so suddenly. Through counseling, our goal was to begin a journey for our emotional healing and recovery.

The sessions allowed us to share our emotions and affirm that what we were experiencing was "normal". The sessions guided us as we sorted out our individual feelings, reactions, and actions to this unexpected reality that we were not ready to accept. The counseling sessions also aided us in respecting each other's unique grief journey. Our counselor also guided us with compromises to consider from the other spouse's perspective. We learned coping mechanisms and strategies that would aid us along the way.

Not only did we seek the expertise of a professional grief counselor, but we also participated in a grief counseling support group called "Grief Share" sponsored by a local church. This group provided safety and a "no judgement" zone" to those who are bereaved by encouraging us to share stories of our loved ones. They provided grief comfort and education from a biblical perspective, which was crucial in not giving up on my faith in God. It was a group for those grieving the loss of parents, children, and friends.

A few months later, we found two grief support groups tailored to parents and siblings. "Compassionate Friends" and "Bereaved Parents" are the groups where we found a deeper level of comfort in sharing about our child. The support groups provide and continue to offer a priceless service for parents, siblings, and families in the community.

Since music has always been an integral part of my life, this was no different now. Every day, I absorbed and embraced encouraging messages found in the comforting words of both old and new gospel songs. Another source of comfort for me was journaling. Every day, I put to paper my vivid memories of my daughter and my dark feelings of despair. I also wrote about my glimpse of hope. Each page provided a release of those feeling from my inner being to the page I was writing on. Once I got it out, those painful feelings no longer consumed me.

For months, I read books on loss. There were even a few books on the loss of a child. I hoped that in reading those books, it would fix the hole in my heart. However, I learned there is no magic wand for grief recovery. One must take it one day at a time and work through the pain. Along the way, I continued to wake up hurt but hopeful.

After Kayla passed, I felt that God had abandoned me. I was angry and hurt. I could not pray for myself. I acknowledge my deep gratitude for family and friends who prayed me through and had me on their minds. I am thankful for their expressions of love with visits, calls, prayers, texts, poems, and flowers that continue to this day.

I distinctly remember spring 2018, and how I began my change from being hurt to having hope. This transitional shift from hurt to hope started with an honest conversation with God. One morning, I threw a tantrum. In prayer, I declared to Him, "I do not understand. I do not like this. I CANNOT MAKE IT THROUGH MY DAY WITHOUT YOUR STRENGTH." The weight of my grief, loss, and pain was too much for me to sustain. I could not carry the weight of my grief by myself. It was too heavy. On the next day before work, I woke up and went to my prayer room. I cried out to the Lord, "I cannot do this anymore by myself. I need you to take this weight. I NEED YOU! I CANNOT DO THIS LIFE I HAVE WITHOUT YOU!" As I wept, cried, wept, and cried, the scripture that came to mind was Psalm 71:20 (The Passion Translation): "Even though you've let us sink down with trials and trouble, I know you will revive us again, lifting us up from the dust of death."

As I released my pain to the Lord, He began to work on me. From that moment, I commenced my day with submission, release, weeping, crying, deep breathing, and worship to God. Daily, some of my heaviness diminished, and some of the "fogginess" faded. With this process came a deeper relationship with God. I confessed my honest emotions to Him no matter how "raw" and no matter how "intense" they were. I was finally able to pray wholeheartedly again for my family, our extended family, friends, and others who were grieving. I asked God for strength for the day. This began my road to healing and recovery of my spiritual tools.

How did I learn to have hope in the midst of my hurt? The answer is by waking up each day and holding on when I did not feel like I had anything to live for. It is not easy to learn to live after someone you love passes away. I made a decision by taking the first step in waking up to embrace my journey with the strength of the Lord and the support of my husband, family, and village. I was not concerned about tomorrow. I learned and became content with getting through the day. My hope was being restored.

Each day, I wake up feeling a little stronger. I am in agreement with the Psalmist in 130:5 New Living Translation: "I am counting on the LORD; yes, I am counting on him. I have put my hope in his word." So, here I am two and a half years later, taking it day by day. As I write these final thoughts through the tears, I confess I am not the same Edana that I was before my Kayla transitioned. I was a strong woman before, but I am a stronger woman now. I am a better wife, mother, sister, friend, and servant. Why? The answer is that I am more compassionate, more appreciative, and do not sweat the small stuff. You may wonder how I how can say that. It is because while losing Kayla was devastating, my love and appreciation for her life have broken me open. I have been hurt, and I am now hopeful. I have experienced loss, and I have experienced love. The love of my husband, my daughter, my son, granddaughters, family, and village envelops me. My love for Kayla never dies. Love still wins! I am indebted to my Kaylalala, who inspires me to "Live, Love, Laff." I am forever #KaylaStrong.

Stephanie Verdieu is the founder and CEO of Intrigue Stylez Hair. From Immigrant to Citizen turning Passion into Purpose. Stephanie entered the United States at the age of 3, not knowing what her circumstances would be in America. Stephanie then found out she had the same privileges as someone who was naturally born in the United States versus being an immigrant. Stephanie learned to braid hair when she was twelve years old and turned her newfound talent into an opportunity, becoming a young entrepreneur earning funds for doing a skill that would later turn into a passion. Her dream of opening a hair salon started in high school. She enrolled in cosmetology school her senior year, intending to open her salon one day. After graduating from cosmetology school, she found a "good job" processing loans for a real estate office. However, she was unhappy and decided to pursue what she truly loved—haircare.

Shortly after getting started in the haircare industry, Stephanie discovered she was pregnant. With all of her responsibilities as a single mother, she thought her dreams of becoming a business owner were a distant memory. Throughout the journey, though, God was there every step of the way. Her paths would cross with Life Coach, Casandra Roache, and Coach Cass took Stephanie on a journey of possibilities. With God, Coach Cass helped to empower Stephanie to step outside of her comfort zone, putting her faith to the test. And here she is, owner and founder of Intrigue Stylez and author of Find Your Outlet and Plug Into It, a tribute to how great God is.

BREAKING THE CYCLE

Have you ever felt stuck, hurt, and confused about moving forward from a painful situation? Were you unable to fathom how you would make it out alive and wondered when the pain would end?

Yeah, I've been in this position more times than I care to count. How was I able to put an end to it, you ask? Because I wanted to be out of the cycle for good. Let me share my story with you.

When the Cycle Began

It started when I was eight years old. I used to hear loud screaming and crying coming from my parents' room. I didn't know why, but I knew my parents were not happy together. Then, one day, I got a glimpse of what was going on, and what I saw left me paralyzed with shock. I witnessed my dad physically abusing my mom, and she was helpless at that moment. I wish I had the courage to help her, but I couldn't move. Tears rolled down my face as I stood there. I remember thinking I would never allow anyone to abuse me in such a way. I made that vow to myself. After that night, I didn't look at my father in the same way. He was now nothing more than an abuser to me. I carried those feelings for a long time.

Pursue with Trauma

Through the years, I was always a scholar student. I was on the honor roll through middle school, and I had my school days planned out. I would keep myself busy in school because home was somewhere I didn't want to be. Memories of that night back when I was eight years old played over and over in my head, and I still felt the anger and fear. Home just wasn't a safe place for me. I was thankful for the friendships I made in school and the after-school programs I was involved with. These friendships helped me to be strong, give back, and strive for a better future. When I graduated from high school, I was excited not just because I was graduating, but also because I was old enough to move out of my parents' house.

I was not able to move out right away because of my legal status in the states. You see, initially, I was not born in the United States. However, during my senior year in high school, I was able to get my Green card through God's grace and everyone who supported my process through immigration. After that process cleared, I was able to get a job finally. With my second paycheck, I found a room to rent and moved out of my parents' house and into the real world.

While working, I also registered for night classes to continue my cosmetology courses so I could get licensed to work in a salon. My teachers told us about a hair show that we should attend, but it was in Georgia. We would have to find our own transportation and hotel. I had a friend who wanted to go. So, we bought the tickets for the hair show, booked the hotel, and rented a car. The following weekend, we left on our way to Georgia. When we got to the hotel, it was beautiful. It was the first time I had left the state. When we got settled into our rooms, we headed to the hair show.

While in the lobby, we ran into the hotel's concierge. He was kind of cute, and he was walking towards us as if we had an "I'm lost" sign on our forehead. He introduced himself, talking with us until the valet brought our car around. He walked us out to the car and told me that he was working the night shift if we needed any help getting around town. I thanked him for his services, and we left the hotel. When we came back that evening, there he was again. He walked us to our room. I stood in the hallway talking with him after my friend said goodnight. We talked for hours until I finally told him that I had to say goodnight. I had to get some sleep for the next day. We exchanged numbers, and I told him that I would keep in touch.

The Trauma Filler and Deception

My new friend and I decided to keep in touch after I left Georgia. We connected on a spiritual level first, and then it went to a romantic relationship. I traveled out of town to see him. We spent time going sightseeing. I fell in love with him and the city. Two years into the relationship, I ended up getting pregnant. That's when his behavior changed drastically. It was like a switch had gone off in his head, and an alarm was sounding in my heart. At first, he denied being the father, and then he came around to the idea of being a father. That should have been a sign that something was off with this man, but I ignored it because I was happy about my pregnancy

It was the day of my baby shower. He had come into town but did not attend the baby shower. Upset, I went to his hotel room. After I walked into the room, I could see that his demeanor was different. Right away, he asked me if I had cheated on him. I looked at him like he was crazy.

We got in a heated argument that night, and the next thing I knew, he pinned me against the wall. Seven months pregnant and pinned to the wall because my boyfriend was insecure. My mind went back to when I saw my father physically abusing my mother. Snapping back to reality, I realized that I had to protect my baby and myself. I pushed him off me, grabbed my keys, and left his hotel room. Nobody knew until this day what transpired that night. I was too hurt to even talk about it with anyone. Of course, he apologized, and I went back to him. I wanted the relationship to work so bad that I allowed my fears to cloud my judgment. He left town and told me to let him know when I went into labor. Ten months pregnant with no job and now living with my family, I felt like I was stuck with nowhere to go. I depended solely on this man to take care of me, which wasn't easy for me.

I was in labor with only my sisters and best friend in the room. He made an excuse that he couldn't leave work right away for his first son's birth. Three days after my son was born, I was at my mother's house. He called and asked could he stay with me.

On Sunday morning, he asked to use my phone, something he would never do. Too tired to argue, I gave it to him. When he later returned my phone, I realized some things were changed and deleted. I got upset at the fact he did this, and he got angry, as well. Another heated argument followed, and we began to physically fight. He put his hand around my throat, choking me. I broke away from him and tore his shirt. When I called my sisters and brothers to come to my rescue, he left when they showed up.

I was left hurt, miserable, and hating that I put myself in that situation again. What was I going to do as a single mom, and how would I manage without an income? My boyfriend apologized, saying he wanted it to work as a family. Crazy as it sounded, I wanted the same thing, too. I didn't want my son to grow up without his father. So, I decided to go along with his plan.

After finding a job, I moved to Georgia. We were two weeks into my living with him when the arguing started. I was clear with myself about what I was not going to tolerate from him. Right before Thanksgiving, it got ugly. I was miserable with my living arrangement, and he did not have much to say to me. The last straw was when I opened the door, and a piece of paper fell to the ground. I realized that was how he had been monitoring my comings and goings. I was very upset and made up my mind that I was going to confront him about it. When I asked him about it, it led to a full-blown argument. He hit me, and I fought back. Of course, he was too strong. I wound up with a twisted ankle. It was then that I knew I had to find a way out of this bad situation.

The Escape from Abuse

After the fight, he was scared to take me to the hospital, afraid of the consequences of his actions. So, he called his family member, who was a nurse, and she brought some crutches over. When she questioned what happened, he lied about how I got hurt, and she believed him. I prayed that night for God to show me a way out of this situation alive and with my son.

My friend was coming into town on Thanksgiving weekend, so I told her to stop by to see me. When she arrived, she saw my condition. She began to ask questions, and I confessed everything. Of course, she wanted me to do something about my situation, but I had no answers for her. After she left, she texted me later in the day to let me know she would be in town for a few more days. If I wanted a way out, she would help me. That's when I put my plan into action.

One night, I knew he would be going to work, and that was the night I packed all my things and left. My friend showed up ready to help, and my neighbors were as well because of all the screaming and crying they heard. I was moving as quickly as I could with a twisted ankle. I was one box away from getting all my stuff in the car, when he showed up early from work. My friend told me to get in the car with the baby so he would not try anything. Trained in self-defense, she was ready to fight if she had to. We called the police, who came quickly and accessed the situation because he accused me of kidnapping my own son. When the police came to my window and asked me what was going on, I told them everything. I was in an abusive relationship, and I wanted out. They asked if I had a place to go, and I told them yes. The police allowed us to go, and that was the day I put a nail end to any abuse in my life.

Lessons and Healing

What's crazy is that what was in my heart manifested in my life. The fear of someone abusing me, and the anger I not only felt against my father but also my son's father. After the whole situation, I moved back to Florida, sought counseling, and built a community around me that was willing to pray for me and encourage me.

It was not easy, and as my son grew up, he started to ask questions and act out. I'm glad I was able to see the hurt in my son, although it was hard to deal with at first. I got a referral from one of my mentors for a child therapist, and we started his sessions when he was eight. You see, I didn't want him growing up with the same trauma that I had gone through, and I did not want to silence his voice as a child either. Counseling helped us grow and acknowledge that we were on the right path.

I thank God that he brought us out of that situation and set us on a new path. I was encouraged to build my business as a cosmetologist and have owned my salon for a few years. My son is almost a teenager now with plans for his own entrepreneurial path. I never look back on that relationship, but God has brought healing. I have forgiven my son's father, and we are able to successfully co-parent our son.

Don't ever allow anyone to cause you to mute your voice, whether it's a boyfriend, husband, family member, or even your boss. Speak up for what's right, and encourage anyone you know, including yourself, to seek help and counseling if they have been abused verbally or physically.

Your identity is found in God and no one else. People come into our lives for seasons or a lifetime. It is up to us, through prayer and communication, to know which one they are assigned to. I knew I had to share my story on how I ended the abuse cycle in my family so that you know you can, too. It might not be abuse that you are dealing with, but there is something you can stand up for and make your voice matter God will see you through it one day at a time.

CPSIA information can be obtained
at www.ICGtesting.com
Printed in the USA
LVHW071502110920
665714LV00014B/1130